C000127881

INVENTIONS

EXTREME FACTS

BY ROBIN TWIDDY

©2019
The Secret Book
Company
King's Lynn
Norfolk PE30 4LS

ISBN: 978-1-912502-39-4

All rights reserved
Printed in Malaysia

Written by:
Robin Twiddy
Edited by:
Kirsty Holmes
Designed by:
Jasmine Pointer

A catalogue record for this book
is available from the British Library.

All facts, statistics, web addresses and URLs in this book were verified as valid and accurate at time of writing.
No responsibility for any changes to external websites or references can be accepted by either the author or publisher.

PHOTO CREDITS

Front cover - Regular, Photoroyalty, Andrii Symonenko, Aleksandra Novakovic, ProStockStudio, jiunn, Jane Kelly, GarikProst, VectorPlotnikoff, focus_bell, Andrew Derr, Art Alex, Colorcocktail, Rvector. 4 - 32 pixels, Luftikus, Rvector, PixMarket. 5 – Flat_Enot, etraveler, krotdesign, bilha Golan, d1sk. 6 – MatiasDelCarmine, ASAG Studio, sunny juice, ironwool, YamabikaY. 7 – kamomeen, Kit8.net, MatiasDelCarmine. 8 – Kwirry, MatiasDelCarmine. 9 - Aleksei Derin, Kwirry. 10 - Mushakesa, bilha Golan. 11 - VectorSun. 12 - marrishuanna, GromovPro, Roi and Roi. 13 – igorrita, Zoltan Major, Mix3r. 14 - ProStockStudio, Sharktailstudio, Grimgram, Anastasia Golubovich. 15 - toranosuke, EVZ, Andrew Rybalko, Olesia Misty. 16 - Natykach Nataliia, tynyuk, ArtMarkova, Lorelyn Medina. 17 - ByEmo, assistant, Olga1818, Tarikdiz. 18 - Nothingelse, Murad_Mammadov, SunshineVector, 4zevar, jehsomwang, Oxy_gen. 19 - Iakov Kalinin. 20 - Dzm1try, Jemastock, johavel, Melody A, Mountain Brothers. 21 - Ivan Dubovik, Top Vector Studio. 22 – Jemastock, Nadya_Art. 23 - Kasa_s, Banana Walking, Andrew Rybalko.

Images are courtesy of Shutterstock.com. With thanks to Getty Images, Thinkstock Photo and iStockphoto.

CONTENTS

Words that look like <u>this</u> can be found in the glossary on page 24.

INVENTIONS THAT CHANGED THE WORLD

The first wheel was invented over 5000 years ago!

3500 BC
First wheel
(Mesopotamia)

2000 BC
First spoked wheel
(Egypt)

1000 BC
First iron rims
(The Celts)

600 BC
First wheelbarrow
(Ancient Greeks)

Paper was first invented in China in **100 BC**.

The nail was invented in ancient Egypt in **3400 BC**.

The printing press was invented by Johannes Gutenberg in 1439. This made books available for everyone for the first time.

Optical lenses were first invented in Mesopotamia and ancient Egypt. They used polished crystal as a magnifying aid.

The glass lens wasn't invented until the Middle Ages.

AD 1845

First air-pumped tyre
RW Thompson)

AD 1893

The Ferris **wheel** (George **Ferris)**

AD 1926

First car **wheel** (Karl Benz)

Nobody invented electricity – it's a natural power source. But **Thomas Edison** worked out how to use it in our homes!

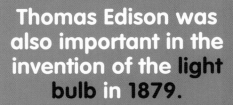

Thomas Edison was also important in the invention of the **light bulb** in 1879.

Many others worked on the light bulb around the same time.

FAMOUS INVENTORS

Thomas Edison (1847 – 1931) had over one **thousand** invention **patents**.

Benjamin Franklin (1706 – 1790) invented <u>bifocal lenses,</u> swim fins, <u>lightning rods</u> and much more.

Stephanie Kwolek (1923 – 2014) invented Kevlar, a very strong material used for bullet-proof vests.

Nikola Tesla (1856 – 1943) developed <u>AC electricity</u>, the <u>Tesla coil</u> and much more.

Hedy Lamarr (1914 – 2000)
invented radio jamming technology, which led to the development of Wi-fi and Bluetooth.

Alexander Graham Bell (1847 – 1922)
invented the telephone and more.

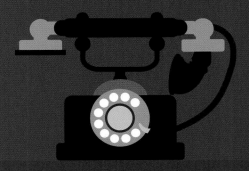

Sir Isaac Newton (1642 – 1726)
invented the reflecting telescope.

Charles Babbage (1791 – 1871)
made the first mechanical computer.

Marie Curie (1867 – 1934)
helped develop the x-ray machine.

LEONARDO DA VINCI

(1452 – 1519)

These are some of the inventions that Da Vinci designed. Many were ahead of their time.

Around 400 years before the Wright brothers, Da Vinci had designed a flying machine!

He had also designed a helicopter-like machine called the aerial screw!

Da Vinci invented an early version of the parachute.

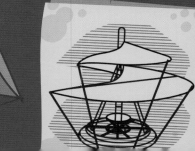

The scuba suit was designed by Da Vinci hundreds of years before anybody else.

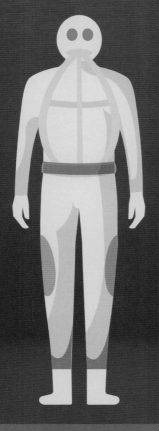

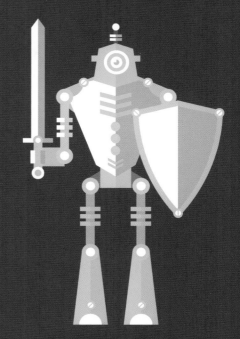

Da Vinci invented a robot knight. This was a suit of armour with gears, weights and pulleys that made it move on its own!

Da Vinci had designed a self-propelling cart roughly 380 years before the first automobile.

FLYING INVENTIONS

Orville and Wilber Wright successfully tested their 'Wright Flyer' on the 17th of December, 1903.

This was the first recorded powered flight ever.

DEC
17

Wilbur and Orville flipped a coin to see who would test the powered flyer first. Wilbur won the toss.

Wilbur's first flight lasted three seconds before he <u>stalled</u> the engine.

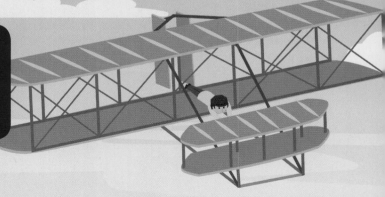

DEC
19

Two days later Orville piloted the flyer over 36 metres at a speed of 11 kilometres per hour (kph).

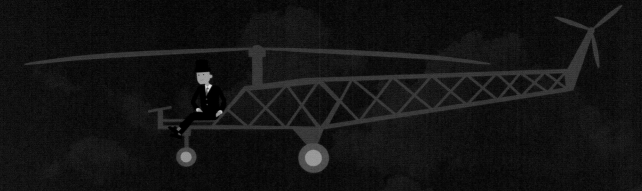

The first successful flight of a helicopter, designed and piloted by Igor Sikorsky, took place on the 13th of May, 1940.

Unmanned drones have been around for nearly 100 years!

Nigel Gifford has invented an <u>edible</u> drone. Every part of the drone can be used for food or shelter. He hopes it will help people all round the world.

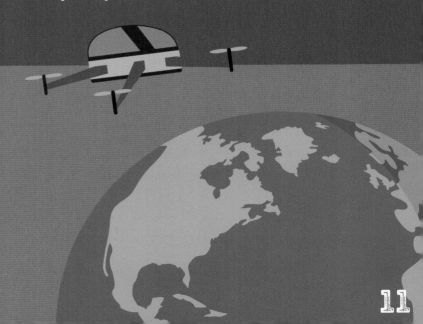

The first drones were radio-controlled planes.

INFORMATION INVENTIONS

These inventions have changed the way that we <u>communicate</u>.

The printing press made sharing information easier, and led to more people learning to read.

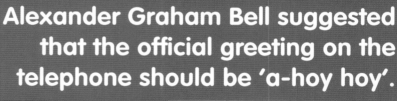

"a-hoy hoy"

Alexander Graham Bell suggested that the official greeting on the telephone should be 'a-hoy hoy'.

In the early 1920s the first mechanical television was invented. It was soon replaced by the much better electronic television in 1927.

The mobile phone was first invented in the early 1970s. It wouldn't be available to the public until the early 1980s.

The first mobile phone available was the DynaTAC 8000X. It offered 30 minutes of talk time, six hours of standby, and could store 30 phone numbers. It cost £2639!

£2639

The DynaTAC 8000X weighed 1.75 pounds. That is roughly four-and-a-half times heavier than a modern smart phone.

COMPUTERS

The first fully-functional computer was the ENIAC. It covered 167 square metres (m), and weighed over 30 tonnes.

A modern <u>microchip</u> the size of a thumbnail can do 30 times more processing than ENIAC could: wow!

The Michigan Micro Mote is the world's smallest computer. It is about one millimetre (mm) <u>cubed</u>. That is about the size of a grain of rice.

The first computer mouse was made out of wood!

Gunpei Yoki invented lots of things for Nintendo **including the Game Boy and the control pad.** He was working as the machine maintenance man when Nintendo's president noticed a toy he had made. Yoki was soon promoted.

The heaviest desktop computer is the **IBM 5120** from 1980. It weighed over 47 kilograms (kg).

Scientists are working on a computer that **uses magnetised water droplets** instead of electronic signals.

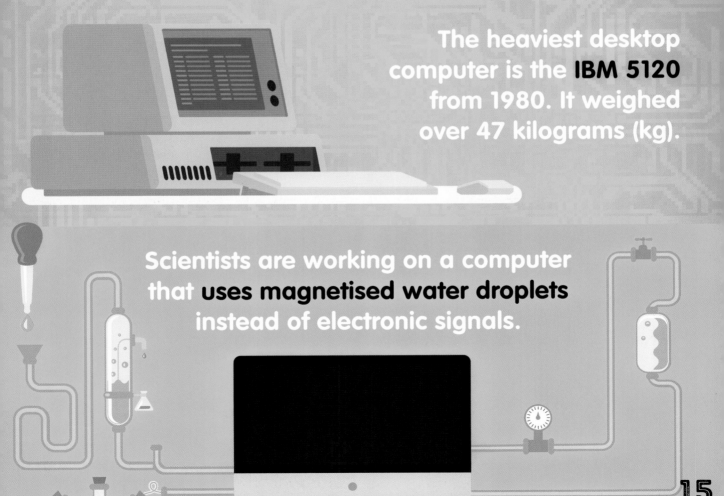

INVENTED BY KIDS

Lots of great things have been invented by kids!

Trampoline: Sixteen-year-old gymnast George Nissen built the first trampoline out of scrap-metal, a canvas bed and rubber springs.

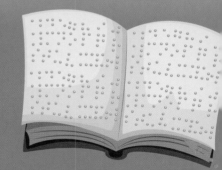

Windsurfing: Peter Chilvers put a sail on his surfboard and invented a new sport when he was twelve!

Braille: Invented by Louis Braille in 1824. He was twelve years old when he invented braille and had been blind since he was three!

Algae Mobile: Fifteen-year-old Param Jaggi created a device that uses algae to change 89% of the CO_2 from cars into oxygen. He hopes that one day all cars will have one.

Ear Muffs: Invented in 1873 by fifteen-year-old Chester Greenwood to keep his ears warm whilst practicing ice skating.

The Snowmobile: Joseph-Armand Bombardier invented the snowmobile in 1922 at the young age of fifteen!

FAILED INVENTIONS

Some inventions just weren't meant to be.

The flying tank.

The Segway was supposed to change personal travel for everyone. The two-wheeled, self-balancing scooter was never really popular.

Twitter Peek launched in 2009. It was a handheld device that only read and posted tweets. Better smartphones soon made this device pointless.

Nikola Tesla once tried to invent a machine that <u>projects</u> your thoughts like a slide show.

In 1985 the C5 battery-and-pedal-powered trike was released. It had no roof, no windscreen, could only carry one person and had a max speed of 24 kph.

When <u>radium</u> was first discovered, people didn't know how dangerous it was. In 1936 you could buy chocolate or bread with radium in it.

In 1887 L. L. Zamenhof unveiled his new language: Esperanto. He believed that it would become a universal language. Over 130 years later it has failed to become the global language Zamenhof wanted it to be.

Learn some Esperanto!
English – 'Hello my name is…'
Esperanto – Saluton mia nomo estas…

ACCIDENTAL INVENTIONS

The Microwave Oven: Whilst wondering what to do with his magnetron (the device used to make microwaves for <u>radars</u>), Percy Spencer noticed his chocolate bar melting… Voilà! The microwave was born!

Artificial Sweeteners: A powder from Constantine Faulberg's lab was still on his hands when he ate his lunch, which tasted very sweet. The sweetener was invented!

Tea Bags: Thomas Sullivan, a tea merchant, sent his tea samples in little silk bags to save money. People thought they were meant to dunk them and started ordering his tea bags!

Crisps: Invented when a chef wanted to play a trick on a customer by making his chips super thin, extra salty and over fried. They turned out to be a hit!

Ice Lollies: Frank Epperson had left a drink with a mixing stick in it outside overnight. In the morning it had frozen, making a flavoured ice lolly!

STRANGE INVENTIONS

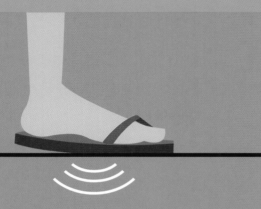

Metal-detecting sandals mean you can search for metal whilst you walk along the beach.

The **corner picture frame** allows you to hang pictures over corners!

Clocky is the alarm clock that runs away from you!

07:30

Doggles are special tinted goggles for dogs!

Air-conditioned trousers have small fans in them to keep you cool!

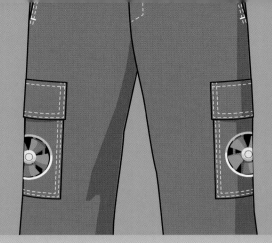

High-tech toilets are mostly found in Japan. These toilets have temperature controls for the <u>bidet</u>, heated seats, self-closing lids, <u>deodorisers</u>, clocks that tell you how long you have been using it and little fans.

In the late 1950s the Bell Company built and tested the first jetpack. It was very dangerous and could only fly for 30 seconds. They called it the rocket belt.

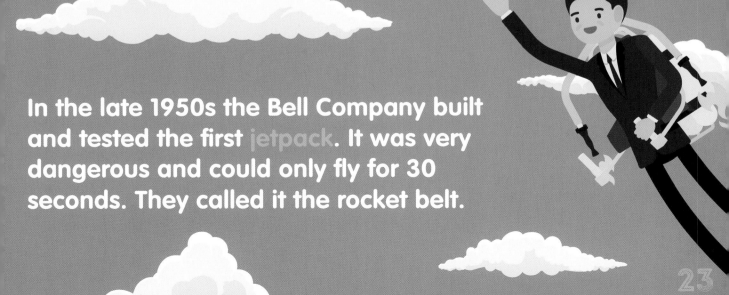

23

GLOSSARY

AC electricity alternating current, where electrons move back and forth rather than round a circuit

algae a plant or plant-like living thing that has no roots, stems, leaves or flowers

artificial something that is man-made

bidet a low sink for washing your bottom after using the toilet

bifocal lenses eye glasses that correct both near and far-sighted problems

communicate to pass information between two or more people

cubed a number that is multiplied by itself three times

deodorisers things that eliminate or cover up odours and smells

edible safe to be eaten

lightning rods grounded metal rods that draw lightning to the ground without hurting anybody

microchip a small silicone device that holds many electrical parts. It helps run computers and other devices

patents a government document that gives the owner the rights to make something they have invented

projects makes an image appear on a surface

radars devices that use radio waves to track objects

radium a radioactive metal which is also a chemical element

stalled when an engine stops unexpectedly

Tesla coil a device that is used to increase alternative current

INDEX